D1716551

INFORMATION
TECHNOLOGY

Exploring Career Pathways

Diane Lindsey Reeves

Created and produced by
Bright Futures Press, Cary, North Carolina
www.brightfuturespress.com

Published by
Cherry Lake Publishing, Ann Arbor, Michigan
www.cherrylakepublishing.com

Photo Credits: Cover, BeautyLine; page 7, Rawpixel.com; Myvisuals; Africa Studio; ra2studio; wavebreakmedia; kurhan; Billion Photos; Audrey Popov; page 8, ra2studio; page 10, kurhan; page 12, Billion Photos; page 14, Africa Studio; page 16, Myvisuals; page 18, Rawpixel.com; page 20, Andrey Popov; page 22, wavebreakmedia; page 24, Ievgenii Meyer.

Library of Congress Cataloging-in-Publication Data

Names: Reeves, Diane Lindsey, 1959- author.
Title: Information technology / Diane Lindsey Reeves.
Description: Ann Arbor, Michigan : Cherry Lake Publishing, 2017. I Series:
    World of work I Includes bibliographical references and index.
Identifiers: LCCN 2016042181I ISBN 9781634726252 (hardcover) I ISBN
    9781634726351 (pdf) I ISBN 9781634726450 (pbk.) I ISBN 9781634726559
    (ebook)
Subjects: LCSH: Information technology--Vocational guideance--Juvenile
    literature. I Computer science--Vocational guidance--Juvenile literature.
Classification: LCC T58.5 .R433 2017 I DDC 004.023--dc23
LC record available at https://lccn.loc.gov/2016042181

Printed in the United States of America.

TABLE OF CONTENTS

HELLO WORLD OF WORK

This is you.

Right now, your job is to go to school and learn all you can.

This is the world of work.

It's where people earn a living, find purpose in their lives, and make the world a better place.

Sooner or later, you'll have to find your way from

HERE to THERE.

To get started, take all the jobs in the incredibly enormous world of work and organize them into an imaginary pile. It's a big pile, isn't it? It would be pretty tricky to find the perfect job for you among so many options.

No worries!

Some very smart career experts have made it easier to figure out. They sorted jobs and industries into groups by the types of skills and products they share. These groups are called career clusters. They provide pathways that will make it easier for you to find career options that match your interests.

Architecture & Construction

Arts & Communications

Business & Administration

Education & Training

Finance

Food & Natural Resources

Government

Health Sciences

Hospitality & Tourism

Human Services

Information Technology

Law & Public Safety

Manufacturing

Marketing

Science, Technology, Engineering & Mathematics (STEM)

Transportation

Good thing you are still a kid.

You have lots of time to explore ideas and imagine yourself doing all kinds of amazing things. The **World of Work** (WoW for short) series of books will help you get started.

TAKE A HIKE!

There are 16 career pathways waiting for you to explore. The only question is: Which one should you explore first?

Is **Information Technology** a good path for you to start exploring career ideas? There is a lot to like about careers in this pathway. It's where the latest and greatest high-tech gadgets we all love to use are imagined, designed, and made. It's where computer apps and video games are created. It's where computer whizzes constantly find new ways to improve businesses and make amazing discoveries with all kinds of technology.

See if any of the following questions grab your interest.

WOULD YOU ENJOY creating your own video game, setting up a Web site, or building your own computer?

CAN YOU IMAGINE someday working at an information technology start-up company, software design firm, or research and development laboratory?

ARE YOU CURIOUS ABOUT what artificial intelligence scientists, big data analysts, computer forensic investigators, software engineers, or video game designers do?

If so, it's time to take a hike! Keep reading to see what kinds of opportunities you can discover along the Information Technology pathway.

But wait!

What if you don't think you'll like this pathway?

You have two choices.

You could keep reading, to find out more than you already know. You might be surprised to learn how many amazing careers you'll find along this path.

OR

Turn to page 27 to get ideas about other WoW pathways.

INFORMATION SECURITY OFFICER

HELP DESK ANALYST

APPLICATION DEVELOPER

E-COMMERCE MANAGER

WoW Up Close

Manage big data. Invent new smartphones. Imagine new software programs and computer applications. Keep computer systems safe from **hackers**. These are just some of the important jobs that people who work along the Information Technology pathway do.

CHIEF INFORMATION OFFICER

VIDEO GAME DESIGNER

SYSTEMS ANALYST

DATA SCIENTIST

APPLICATION DEVELOPER

There's an app for that! For what, you ask? There are computer and smartphone software **applications** for just about anything you can imagine. Learn a new language? Find the perfect pet? Get help with your homework? Yes, yes, and yes!

Have you ever heard of Google? Facebook? Netflix? These apps are so popular and so widely used that you may not even realize you are using a computer app. Other apps make life easier in many ways. For instance, the ATM (automatic teller machine) your parents use to get some quick cash are powered by apps. So are the "shopping carts" in all your favorite online stores.

There are millions of apps out there, and faster, smarter, and cooler ones are coming out every day. The one thing they all have in common is that they were created by **application developers**. They come up with the ideas for computer and software applications. Then they design and program them. The work requires equal parts of creative talent and technical skill.

Application developers typically have a **bachelor's degree** in computer science and experience in programming. The work pays well, and there are lots of opportunities waiting for future application developers. It's a field where you can develop fun and games and develop apps to solve real world problems too.

Check It Out!

Get acquainted with a young computer app developer at

▶ http://bit.ly/KIdApp

Use the Internet to search for other young computer whizzes using the search term "kid computer app developer."

Start Now!

- ✔ Make a list of all the computer applications you and your family use on a regular basis.

- ✔ Keep up with the latest kid-friendly computer apps by using your favorite search engine to look for "best apps for kids" and "best educational apps."

- ✔ Sketch out ideas for a computer app you'd like to create.

CHIEF INFORMATION OFFICER

Maybe you've heard of a chief executive officer or CEO. That's the person who is the biggest boss of a company. A **chief information officer**, or CIO, is the biggest boss of a company's technology.

It is the CIO's job to make sure that every employee in the company has the technology tools and knowledge to do their jobs as efficiently as possible. This, of course, involves making decisions about what types of technology the company will use.

MacBooks or PCs? Laptops or desktops? It can be tempting to bring in all the latest gizmos and gadgets. But a CIO has to make smart decisions about what it really takes to get the job done. Busting the budget to buy new laptops just because they come in cool colors doesn't cut it!

An even bigger part of a CIO's job is figuring out the best ways for the company to use technology. CIOs make decisions about the systems and software a company uses. They figure out ways to use those systems and that software to make the business run smoothly and successfully. They also make sure that employees know how to use these resources in ways that make their jobs easier.

Check It Out!

Use the search terms "history of technology" and "technology trends" to seek out online information about how technology has evolved over time. Try to imagine what might come next!

Start Now!

- ✓ Think about getting involved in student government to gain some leadership experience.

- ✓ Join the school computer club to stay up with the latest technologies.

- ✓ Make a timeline of the different types of technologies your family has used since you were born. Your parents can clue you in about what they were using when you were too young to notice.

DATA SCIENTIST

Big data is big. Some experts say that more data has been created in the past two years than in the entire previous history of the human race. Now that's BIG data!

Data, by the way, is bits of information. For instance, when you go online to Netflix and download movies and binge on favorite TV shows, you leave behind bits of information about your choices. Multiply this by the millions of people who use Netflix and you have millions of bits of data. And, presto, you have an example of big data. Netflix uses this data to make decisions about what kinds of shows to offer to its customers.

So what's the big deal about big data? **Data scientists** use big data to help businesses do a better job of whatever it is that they do. Sports teams use it to analyze athletes' performances. Retail stores use it to market products to their customers. Health researchers use it to search for causes of and cures for diseases. The potential for big data is HUGE.

It is up to data scientists to find meaning in all the data and help others figure out how to use it in helpful ways. They use statistics, **algorithms**, and computer modeling to **analyze** data and make sense of it. Data scientists must have strong software engineering and analytical skills.

Check It Out!

What is big data? Find out online at

▶ http://bit.ly/BigDataIntro

▶ http://bit.ly/BigDataHealthy

▶ http://bit.ly/BigDataChange

Start Now!

✓ Playing video games? Doing homework? Using social media? Make a chart to keep track of how you use your online time for an entire week. What apps do you use on a regular basis?

✓ Take a survey among your friends and classmates to find out about their favorite apps.

E-COMMERCE MANAGER

There was a time when, if you wanted to buy something, you had to go to an actual store to get it. Technology has changed all that.

Now, people can shop in stores located all over the world from the comfort of their own homes. All they need is an Internet connection and a credit card. This is called e-commerce.

E-commerce managers make these online shopping experiences happen. These tech-savvy professionals do some of the same things that the managers of "brick and mortar" stores at your local mall do. Running a store in cyberspace brings different kinds of responsibilities, too.

First, e-commerce managers must get their online stores up and running. They have to make the Web site look good, run smoothly, and be a safe place for customers to make purchases. Speaking of customers, a big part of an e-commerce manager's job is attracting them to the Web site with attention-grabbing social media marketing. Then it's all about getting those customers to come back for more great products and excellent customer service.

Cha-ching!

Check It Out!

Go online and find the Web site for your favorite brand of

- ▶ Fast food
- ▶ Shampoo
- ▶ Blue jeans
- ▶ Sneakers
- ▶ Cars

Start Now!

- ✔ Pick a favorite store. Think about what it is like to actually visit and shop in that store. Then go online to visit the store's Web site. Make a chart to compare the similarities and differences.

- ✔ Use pictures from magazines or the Internet to create a catalog of products you would want to sell in your own online store.

HELP DESK ANALYST

Have you ever tried to explain how to use a computer or smartphone to your parents or grandparents? If so, you can understand the communication skill and oodles of patience it takes to explain something complicated to someone who is, um, kind of clueless.

Take that situation and make it a couple thousand times more complicated. Then you'll have an idea of what **help desk analysts** do. Some work directly with consumers (like your parents or grandparents) helping them figure out how to use a specific computer program or technology tool. In some cases, they can actually get into a consumer's computer system and work out problems from a distance.

In other cases, help desk analysts work with business clients to help them operate entire software systems. Their job is to identify problems and work out solutions. **Glitches** happen and people make mistakes. A help desk analyst has to know a lot about computers to identify the source of the problem. It's like being a computer expert, technology teacher, and troubleshooter all wrapped up in one.

Help desk analysts don't wear capes and tights like other superheroes. But they save the day for many technology users.

Check It Out!

Ever wonder how to do or make something? Visit the how-to experts at

 http://www.ehow.com

Start Now!

- ✓ Volunteer to help younger students figure out how to use computers in the school computer lab or media center.

- ✓ Imagine that you had to teach an alien from outer space how to use e-mail. Make a poster showing the step-by-step process.

- ✓ Pay extra attention in your technology class and notice the things your teacher does to help kids learn to use computers.

INFORMATION SECURITY OFFICER

Information security officers are like cyber cops. Instead of using handcuffs and sirens, they use computer knowledge and detection skills to solve and stop **cybercrimes**.

Millions of people have personal information online. This includes financial information like bank accounts and credit cards. Businesses of all sizes have trade secrets and business data online. Governments use computers to store and communicate all kinds of super sensitive information. Vital community services like hospitals, power plants, and 9-1-1 systems rely on computer systems to do their important work.

When this sensitive information gets into the wrong hands, it can cause big problems. It doesn't matter if it's an individual or a government agency. Money can be lost. Secrets leaked. Services messed up. In some cases, it can put people's lives at risk.

Hackers are one of the biggest threats to computer safety. Hackers are people who secretly get access to a computer system in order to get information and cause damage. Information security officers track down hackers and shut them down. They create **firewalls** and install security software to keep information safe. They also monitor networks to identify attacks and respond to alerts.

Check It Out!

Play around with cyber safety at

▶ http://pbskids.org/ webonauts

▶ http://www. carnegiecyberacademy.com

▶ http://bit.ly/FTCOnGuard

Start Now!

✓ Make up a set of flash cards you could use to teach younger kids about cyber safety.

✓ Solve some cybercrimes at the FBI's Cyber Surf Island at https://sos.fbi.gov.

✓ Make sure you use strong passwords to protect your online information.

SYSTEMS ANALYST

Systems analysts are experts in both computers and business. Their first job is to understand their client's or employer's business. Their second job is to use the best technologies—software, hardware, and networks—to help the business succeed.

Systems analysts work for all kinds of businesses in all kinds of fields, including information technology (IT), science, health care, and banking. In fact, so many businesses need their help that the U.S. Department of Labor says there will be lots of jobs for systems analysts in the future. Systems analysts rank high on many lists of best IT jobs. That's because the job pays well, is low stress, and offers lots of opportunities.

Systems analysts do for businesses what doctors do for sick patients. Doctors figure out why their patients are unhealthy and recommend ways to make them healthy again. Systems analysts figure out how businesses work and recommend ways to make them work even better. There is quite a bit of variety in the types of tasks that systems analysts do. So there is little chance of getting bored on the job!

Preparing for this type of work requires a bachelor's degree in information science. It also helps to go on to acquire a **master's degree** in business administration. That way you have both the computer and business knowledge you need to do an amazing job.

Check It Out!

Go online to see what you can find out about "how computers work" and "how business works."

Start Now!

✔ Make a flowchart showing how computers work.

✔ Look at the ways your family gets ready for school and work in the morning. Then make (polite!) recommendations on how to improve the process for everyone.

✔ Find out if your school has a computer or business club and join one.

Property Of
Wisconsin School for the

VIDEO GAME DESIGNER

You mean people get paid to play video games? Well, someone has to create all those cool Xbox games you love to play on computers, smartphones, and TVs. Those lucky "someones" are **video game designers**.

Video game designers are part of a team that creates and develops video games. On the creative side, they come up with the game idea and rules. The team also creates the game's characters, setting, and story. Then comes the technical part, where programmers write code and use special computer software to script out the commands that create the action.

It can take months and even years to create complex video games. Some of the most popular, like *Minecraft*, *Wii Sports*, and *Super Mario Bros.*, cost millions of dollars and enormous amounts of talent to produce.

Video game designers usually need a college degree in video game design or computer science. Future video game designers (like you?) can start getting ready by taking computer programming and graphic design courses. You can also explain that your constant desire to play video games is actually career research. At least, you can try to convince your parents or teachers that's why you play so many games. There's no guarantee that anyone will buy the excuse!

Check It Out!

Create your own stories, games, and animations at

 https://scratch.mit.edu

Start Now!

☑ Play games online at popular Web sites like Nickelodeon (http://www.nick.com/games) and Disney (http://disneychannel.disney.com/games).

☑ Make a list of your favorite video game characters and features.

☑ Create a storyboard of your ideas for an awesome new video game.

APPLICATION DEVELOPER • Business intelligence analyst • Business intelligence manager • Business process analyst • Cartographer • Channel supervisor • **CHIEF INFORMATION OFFICER** • Computer-aided design (CAD) programmer • Computer-aided manufacturing (CAM) programmer • Computer hardware engineer • Computer network architect • Computer numerically controlled machine tool programmer • Computer operator • Computer programmer • Computer science teacher • Computer scientist • Control system manager • Database administrator • Database architect • Database

WoW Big List

Take a look at some of the different kinds of jobs people do in the Information Technology pathway. **WoW!**

Some of these job titles will be familiar to you. Others will be so unfamiliar that you will scratch your head and say "huh?"

consultant • **DATA SCIENTIST** • Data security administrator • Data warehousing manager • Director of enterprise strategy • Document management specialist • **E-COMMERCE MANAGER** • Enterprise content manager • Geographical information systems director • Geospatial information scientist • Global intelligence analyst • Graphic designer • **HELP DESK ANALYST** • Information architect •

Information modeling engineer • Information research scientist • Information security analyst • **INFORMATION SECURITY OFFICER** • Information technology manager • Internet marketing consulting • JAVA developer • Local area network administrator • Multimedia artist • Network analyst • Network technician • Programmer analyst • Project manager • Quality assurance analyst • Records manager • Registered communication distribution designer • Resource manager • Search engine optimization manager • Software developer • Software engineer • Software quality assurance engineer • Software

Find a job title that makes you curious. Type the name of the job into your favorite Internet search engine and find out more about the people who have that job.

1 What do they do?

2 Where do they work?

3 How much training do they need to do this job?

quality assurance tester • Software test engineer • **SYSTEMS ANALYST** • Systems architect • Systems engineer • Technical project lead • Technical support specialist • Telecom network manager • Telecommunications engineer • Telecommunications systems designer • Video game creative director • **VIDEO GAME DESIGNER** • Web administrator • Webmaster • Web programmer

TAKE YOUR PICK

	Put stars next to your 3 favorite career ideas	Put an X next to the career idea you like the least	Put a question mark next to the career idea you want to learn more about
Application Developer			
Chief Information Officer			
Data Scientist			
E-commerce Manager			
Help Desk Analyst			
Information Security Officer			
Systems Analyst			
Video Game Designer			
	What do you like most about these careers?	What is it about this career that doesn't appeal to you?	What do you want to learn about this career? Where can you find answers?

Which Big Wow List ideas are you curious about?

EXPLORE SOME MORE

The Information Technology pathway is only one of 16 career pathways that hold exciting options for your future. Take a look at the other 15 to figure out where to start exploring next.

Architecture and Construction

WOULD YOU ENJOY making things with LEGOs™, building a treehouse or birdhouse, or designing the world's best skate park?

CAN YOU IMAGINE someday working at a construction site, a design firm, or a building company?

ARE YOU CURIOUS ABOUT what civil engineers, demolition technicians, heavy-equipment operators, landscape architects, or urban planners do?

Arts & Communications

WOULD YOU ENJOY drawing your own cartoons, using your smartphone to make a movie, or writing articles for the student newspaper?

CAN YOU IMAGINE someday working at a Hollywood movie studio, a publishing company, or a television news station?

ARE YOU CURIOUS ABOUT what actors, bloggers, graphic designers, museum curators, or writers do?

Business & Administration

WOULD YOU ENJOY playing Monopoly, being the boss of your favorite club or team, or starting your own business?

CAN YOU IMAGINE someday working at a big corporate headquarters, government agency, or international business center?

ARE YOU CURIOUS ABOUT what brand managers, chief executive officers, e-commerce analysts, entrepreneurs, or purchasing agents do?

Education & Training

WOULD YOU ENJOY babysitting, teaching your grandparents how to use a computer, or running a summer camp for neighbor kids in your backyard?

CAN YOU IMAGINE someday working at a college counseling center, corporate training center, or school?

ARE YOU CURIOUS ABOUT what animal trainers, coaches, college professors, guidance counselors, or principals do?

Finance

WOULD YOU ENJOY earning and saving money, being the class treasurer, or playing the stock market game?

CAN YOU IMAGINE someday working at an accounting firm, bank, or Wall Street stock exchange?

ARE YOU CURIOUS ABOUT what accountants, bankers, fraud investigators, property managers, or stockbrokers do?

Food & Natural Resources

WOULD YOU ENJOY exploring nature, growing your own garden, or setting up a recycling center at your school?

CAN YOU IMAGINE someday working at a national park, raising crops in a city farm, or studying food in a laboratory?

ARE YOU CURIOUS ABOUT what landscape architects, chefs, food scientists, environmental engineers, or forest rangers do?

Government

WOULD YOU ENJOY reading about U.S. presidents, running for student council, or helping a favorite candidate win an election?

CAN YOU IMAGINE someday working at a chamber of commerce, government agency, or law firm?

ARE YOU CURIOUS about what mayors, customs agents, federal special agents, intelligence analysts, or politicians do?

Health Sciences

WOULD YOU ENJOY nursing a sick pet back to health, dissecting animals in a science lab, or helping the school coach run a sports clinic?

CAN YOU IMAGINE someday working at a dental office, hospital, or veterinary clinic?

ARE YOU CURIOUS ABOUT what art therapists, doctors, dentists, pharmacists, and veterinarians do?

Hospitality & Tourism

WOULD YOU ENJOY traveling, sightseeing, or meeting people from other countries?

CAN YOU IMAGINE someday working at a convention center, resort, or travel agency?

ARE YOU CURIOUS ABOUT what convention planners, golf pros, tour guides, resort managers, or wedding planners do?

Human Services

WOULD YOU ENJOY showing a new kid around your school, organizing a neighborhood food drive, or being a peer mediator?

CAN YOU IMAGINE someday working at an elder care center, fitness center, or mental health center?

ARE YOU CURIOUS ABOUT what elder care center directors, hairstylists, personal trainers, psychologists, or religious leaders do?

Law & Public Safety

WOULD YOU ENJOY working on the school safety patrol, participating in a mock court trial at school, or coming up with a fire escape plan for your home?

CAN YOU IMAGINE someday working at a cyber security company, fire station, police department, or prison?

ARE YOU CURIOUS ABOUT what animal control officers, coroners, detectives, firefighters, or park rangers do?

 ## Manufacturing

WOULD YOU ENJOY figuring out how things are made, competing in a robot-building contest, or putting model airplanes together?

CAN YOU IMAGINE someday working at a high-tech manufacturing plant, engineering firm, or global logistics company?

ARE YOU CURIOUS ABOUT what chemical engineers, industrial designers, supply chain managers, robotics technologists, or welders do?

 ## Marketing

WOULD YOU ENJOY keeping up with the latest fashion trends, picking favorite TV commercials during Super Bowl games, or making posters for a favorite school club?

CAN YOU IMAGINE someday working at an advertising agency, corporate marketing department, or retail store?

ARE YOU CURIOUS ABOUT what creative directors, market researchers, media buyers, retail store managers, and social media consultants do?

 ## Science, Technology, Engineering & Mathematics (STEM)

WOULD YOU ENJOY concocting experiments in a science lab, trying out the latest smartphone, or taking advanced math classes?

CAN YOU IMAGINE someday working in a science laboratory, engineering firm, or research and development center?

ARE YOU CURIOUS ABOUT what aeronautical engineers, ecologists, statisticians, oceanographers, or zoologists do?

 ## Transportation

WOULD YOU ENJOY taking pilot or sailing lessons, watching a NASA rocket launch, or helping out in the school carpool lane?

CAN YOU IMAGINE someday working at an airport, mass transit system, or shipping port?

ARE YOU CURIOUS ABOUT what air traffic controllers, flight attendants, logistics planners, surveyors, and traffic engineers do?

MY WoW

I am here.

Name _____

Grade _____

School _____

Who I am.

Make a word collage! Use 5 adjectives to form a picture that describes who you are.

Where I'm going.

The next career pathway I want to explore is

_____

Some things I need to learn first to succeed.

1 _____

2 _____

3 _____

My Career Choice

To get here.

GLOSSARY

algorithms
processes or sets of rules to be followed in calculations or other problem-solving operations, especially by a computer

analyze
to examine something carefully in order to understand it

application
a computer program designed to perform a group of coordinated functions, tasks, or activities for the benefit of the user

application developer
person who translates software requirements into workable programming code to develop programs for use with computers, smartphones, and other technologies

bachelor's degree
a degree that is given to a student by a college or university usually after four years of study

chief information officer
person in charge of the strategy and the computer systems required to support a business or organization

cybercrime
criminal activity or a crime that involves the Internet, a computer system, or computer technology

data scientist
person who analyzes large amounts of data to help a business gain a competitive edge

e-commerce manager
person who oversees a retail company's online sales and presence

firewalls
software designed to control access to a computer in order to protect it from outside attacks

glitches
sudden things that go wrong or cause a problem, usually with machinery like computers

hacker
someone who has a special skill for getting into a computer system without permission

help desk analyst
person who provides technical support for any aspect of the information systems department

information security officer
person responsible for the security of a company's communications and other business systems

information technology
all the jobs involved in the design, development, support, and management of computer hardware, software, multimedia, and other systems

master's degree
a degree that is given to a student with a bachelor's degree for an additional year or two of college studies

systems analyst
person who specializes in analyzing, designing, and implementing information systems

video game designer
person who plans, designs, and creates video games

INDEX

* Refers to the Web page sources

About the Author

Diane Lindsey Reeves is the author of lots of children's books. She has written several original PEANUTS stories (published by Regnery Kids and Sourcebooks). She is especially curious about what people do and likes to write books that get kids thinking about all the cool things they can be when they grow up. She lives in Cary, North Carolina, and her favorite thing to do is play with her grandkids—Conrad, Evan, Reid, and Hollis Grace.